RAY COMFORT

101 Things Husbands Do to Annoy Their Wives

Bridge-Logos *Publishers*

Gainesville, Florida 32614 USA

101 Things Husbands Do to Annoy Their Wives

Bridge-Logos Publishers
P.O. Box 141630
Gainesville, FL 32614, USA
www.bridgelogos.com

ISBN 0-88270-956-9

Edited by Lynn Copeland

Cover, page design, and production by Genesis Group
Printed in the United States of America

To my wonderful wife,
Sue,
...who helped me write
this book in ten minutes

My sincere thanks to:
Daren Streblow, Kirk Cameron,
Emeal Zwayne, Kevin Kickham, Timm Smith,
Greg Bush, Garry Ansdell, Jed Seneca,
Dan Moulton, Mike Smalley, David Price,
Chuck Thoele, Jesse Gonzales, Harry Brut,
Jimmy Vargas, and Jerry Loveall (and their
wives) for their valuable input.
Special thanks to Rachel Zwayne, Daniel
Comfort, Claudia Emmerson, Jacob Comfort,
and Walt and Joc Greeman.

Contents

1

*He walks
too quickly
through malls.*

Explanation:

A man is able to shop with a woman (looking at feminine things) for a maximum of fifteen seconds. At that point a chemical called epinephrine (similar to adrenaline) is released within his body. This powerful substance makes him want to either run or fall into a deep sleep. This disorder is known as *mallcolepsy*.

Any shopping with a woman may cause him to manifest symptoms of this disorder. He will become anxious and fidgety. Sweat may develop on his upper lip, and he will utter short hurry-up phrases like, "Okay, then . . . ," and, "Well, that's that, then."

An antidote to this disturbing condition is to put him in the company of one or more males who are looking at high-tech electronics, sporting goods, or camera equipment. Or just let him fall asleep under a rack of clothing.

USA Today *reported that a woman who called 911 faced the possibility of 18 months in jail. Her reason for calling the emergency number was that her husband wouldn't go shopping with her.*

2

He doesn't listen when she is talking to him.

Explanation:

The key to communication with a man is to watch his eyes. If the eyes are in a dreamlike state, the brain is processing other (what he considers *more important*) data. At this point, any sounds coming from his mouth, such as "Uh-huh," mean nothing. These are the symptoms of CDD: Communication Deficit Disorder.

Men *rarely* hear information the first time. CDD is caused by the location of the male inner ear, which prevents initial details from penetrating the brain. They merely remain in the *porch* of the outer ear. A sign that the details are still in the porch will be the word "Huh?" or "What?" uttered 5 to 15 seconds (sometimes up to 60 seconds) after the information is given. This indicates he has merely heard a *background noise*.

Information must be expressed at least twice (the second time with more resolve), followed by the words, *"Are you listening to me?"* This should effectively move the data from the porch to the inner ear (which is connected directly to the brain). Science informs us that women speak twice as much as men. This is because men need to be told things twice.

Studies reveal that men speak 13,000 words a day. Women speak approximately 25,000 words.

3

He calls people by the wrong name.

Explanation:

This tends to embarrass a woman, only because she doesn't understand that this is the natural developmental process of the English language. When a man calls Mark "Mike," or Mike "Mark," he is beginning this amazing process. Take for instance Robert. His close friends call him "Bob." William is called "Bill," and Richard's friends call him "Dick."

Ask yourself who would have first called Robert "Bob," William "Bill," and Richard "Dick." The odds are that it was a man who began this important progression of the English language. There are not many women who have two completely different names. This is probably because women lack this natural gifting—the remarkable ability that men possess—to bring "color" to their native tongue by substituting names that are totally distinct from the original.

Men often embarrass their wives. Tim Berrends (a popular radio talk show host) and his wife were eating at a restaurant when a man near them began to choke on his food. Tim immediately stood to his feet and in a loud voice asked, "Does anyone know the Hemlock maneuver?" No one did. Neither did anyone know the famous Heimlich maneuver, so Tim tried it . . . and it worked.

4

He says, "Shhhhh" while watching television.

Explanation:

The sound "Shhhhh" is commonly considered to be a byproduct of the cruel and harsh "Shut-up!" However, every husband knows that "Shhhhh" is actually a shortened derivative of:

"Shhhhhweetheart...I love you so much. But at the present moment this powerful TV program has my ever-loving mind in its grip. I'm not made like you. The left side of my brain can take in only one body of information at once. Therefore, I have made a calculated choice to deny myself the joy of your immediate communication. This is so that I can watch this program, and then share its excitement with you in a few moments. I hope you don't mind, shhhhhweetheart."

5

He dreams while driving.

Explanation:

The male mind is intensely creative, and it is the sound of the vehicle engine turning over that turns over his finely tuned machine of the mind—that powerfully complex computer of computers. All she sees is a vacant look in his eyes, and she wrongly concludes that he is off in a dream. But he *is* in total control.

Who knows the depths of intelligence into which he is drilling—searching for the oil of creativity, believing that one day he will strike it rich ... and make this world a better place for both him and his beloved family.

One well-known preacher, who was in total control, finished his sermon and went down to mingle with his listeners. He approached a woman in the front row who had a blanket across her, covering what was obviously a small child. As he leaned down, he pulled back the blanket and warmly said, "My, what have we here?" She was breast-feeding.

6

He snatches what she's reading out of her hands, so he can read it.

Explanation:

With a little probing, it will be discovered that what appears to be impatience happens only with certain types of written information—news. This *snatching* (for want of a better word) occurs only because he knows that the female mind *needs* details. She will therefore take quite some time to finish her information-gathering process. Until then, time for him seems to stand still. He is fully aware that tomorrow's news is not news. His central nervous system suddenly craves *immediate* knowledge—*while it is still news*—and this dominant instinct overtakes his ability to cope with any prolonged delay. This is known as Male Introactive Analysis Syndrome.

He says, "Yes, dear."

Explanation:

This is not (as it often seems) a phrase that carries implications of nagging. It is just that the low-pitched male voice has difficulty communicating a sincere tone to the sensitive female ear with such a short phrase.

A pastor in Phoenix, Arizona, recently felt what it's like to be a woman speaking to a man. When he placed his order at a restaurant's drive-thru, he didn't even get a "Yes, dear." There was no response. So he gave the order again, this time in a louder voice. When there was still no acknowledgment, he impatiently leaned out of his car window to give the order once again, and saw that he had been talking to a trash bin.

8

He snores with his mouth open.

Explanation:

The creative mind in a man needs oxygen to function. An open mouth gives entry to the maximum amount of this most necessary fuel. The unique sound of the snoring is his way of letting her know that he is in the depths of his creative mode, and therefore should *never* be disrupted.

Sadly, many an unenlightened woman has thumped her husband in the night during this process, depriving humanity of what may have been remarkable inventions and creative ideas...as well as causing him to forget important dates.

In Florida, a 54-year-old man may have another reason for why men snore. When he went to the doctor to have his nasal passages cleared, the doctor removed a cherry pit that had been lodged there for 50 years. When he was 4 years old, the man pushed the pit up his nose and forgot all about it.

9

He makes jokes about her mother.

Explanation:

Men skydive. They risk life and limb by riding the backs of wild beasts. They climb jagged peaks. They are by nature driven to live "on the edge." *They crave the adrenaline rush.* Most men haven't the time to break away from their daily responsibilities to carry out these strong aspirations. They therefore get their rush (their flirt with death) by making mother-in-law jokes.

10

He doesn't ask for directions when lost.

Explanation:

Lost people ask for directions. Men *never* get lost. They are merely *finding their way*. This often takes time and distance. Magellan, Columbus, James Cook, etc., no doubt *seemed* lost until they found their way to new lands.

County police in Fairfax, Virginia, thought their police car had been lost through theft. However, they withdrew an all-points bulletin for the missing vehicle. It turned out that a police detective had taken the unmarked car home and left it in his driveway while he was out of town.

11

He walks away while she's talking to him.

Explanation:

This phenomenon often occurs for two reasons. First, the male must process important facts as soon as they pass from the outer ear into the inner ear, and then into the brain. To do this effectively, he must immediately seek a place of peace and quiet. She may get the impression that he is impatient, rude, insensitive, and uncaring, when he is actually wanting to go and digest the meaningful information he has already received.

Second, almost all men want to be leaders. Their dream is to have the admiration of their wives. Often, the husband will begin this important process while he has her attention—*while she is speaking to him.* It is at this time that he takes the lead, hoping that she will follow.

12

He leaves the plastic ties off the bread.

Explanation:

Few women know how it feels for a man to have to wear a necktie. It may *look* good, but a tie around the throat of a male epitomizes the 9-to-5 rush of the modern lifestyle. It stands for freeway traffic, the rat race, the tension, pressures, frustrations, and stress of daily living in a "plastic" world.

Empathy drives him to want to see that the bread is freed from having its neck tied. Instead, he gently twists the bag and places it safely in the bread box.

13

He puts food in the microwave and doesn't cover it.

Explanation:

The failure to cover food in a microwave is actually a case of consideration for his wife. She can instantly see what foods need to be replaced in the cupboard, simply by looking at the cuisine splattered all over the inside of the microwave.

14

He drives against the arrows in a parking lot.

Explanation:

What may look like mere paint and arrows to a woman is *war paint* and *"Indians!"* to a man. *This is no time to listen to the screams of a hysterical woman.* He must keep his head (scalp) in the face of many arrows. His hands grip the reins. Horsepower throbs under the hood. He must keep the wheels turning, circle his wagon, and bring his beloved family to a place of safety.

An 86-year-old woman drove against the arrows for 15 miles at 37 mph on Interstate 80 near Sparks, Nevada, before a state trooper forced a minor collision near the California state line. The woman's driver's license restrictions included no freeway driving. No injuries were reported.

15

He rips off 26 paper towels to dry his hands.

Explanation:

N ot many women understand the challenge of a bullfight. The proud matador stands before a subdued beast and, with great magnificence, flashes his paper-like cape through the air. This is what is behind the strong thrust with which a *real* man pulls at paper towels. The *whirring* noise of the roller sounds to his tuned ear like the deep snorting of a bull in absolute subjection.

In Melbourne, Florida, a would-be robber tried to rip off a store's cash register. But the store owner refused to hand over the keys to the register—even with a gun held to his head. The frustrated robber then picked up the cash register and ran out of the store. Unfortunately, he forgot to unplug it, and it was ripped from his hands as he ran out the door. By this time, the owner had located a baseball bat. He chased the robber, smashed his car windshield, and wrote down the license plate as he drove away. The shaken man was arrested a short time later.

16

He asks her to get to the point when she's explaining something.

Explanation:

Men like to read the headlines *before* they commit themselves to the fine print. Women, in their wonderful uniqueness, tend to give the fine print *first*.

This is how to captivate the male mind: Instead of saying,

> "Honey, do you know that bank on High Street—the one with the large front window with the ugly frame...where Martha's husband, Eric, worked for eleven years before his brother ran off with his secretary and put him in financial strife? He had to resign from that bank. He was actually *forced* to hand in his notice, because of the money he lost when his brother invested it for him in a 'sure thing'...*was he bad news!* I knew it the first time I met him. Now Eric works at the power board...has done so since 1992...by the way, she's pregnant again. Martha, that is. Sweet girl.—Well, it was robbed!"

Rather, begin with the headline: "The High Street bank was robbed!" Then, if he is interested, he will listen to the details.

17

He drinks directly from the milk container.

Explanation:

Not only does he avoid dirtying a glass, but a man knows that bacteria tend to accumulate around the openings of liquid containers. When he places his lips on the container opening, he is willingly making a sacrifice for his family. The removal of bacteria means health and strength for his loved ones.

18

He tells her to hurry when she's doing her hair.

Explanation:

H is "Hurry up!" is actually childlike excitement to see the finished product. If you look closely, he may even be clenching his fists (like an excited little child) when he says this.

19

He waits until they are about to go out before mentioning a loose button.

Explanation:

War makes heroes. Pressure often brings out the best in humanity. Painful though it may be, to spring things onto her at the last moment will bring out the best in her... something he *loves* to see.

20

He falls asleep while watching TV.

Explanation:

S omething he has seen on television has sent
him into his *creative mode* (see explanation
#8).

21

He stands around the kitchen when she is cooking.

Explanation:

His lifting the pot lids and poking at the food is merely a pretense. He is there just to be close to her.

22

He whistles the same tune 400 times.

Explanation:

This is another case of the outer and inner ear syndrome (see explanation #2). The high pitch of the whistle isn't able to penetrate his inner ear, so each time he whistles the tune, it sounds as fresh to him as the first time. This can be seen as a blessing, rather than a curse.

Geoffrey O'Neill, from Essex in England, has been whistling on the porch for more than twenty years. That's how long he's been writing what he calls "catchy tunes that people remember and whistle." During that time, he wrote over 500 tunes, none of which were published. Number 332 was called "People Think I'm Stupid."

23

He yawns in public without putting his hand over his mouth.

Explanation:

Like the snore, the yawn is the body's way of pulling in necessary oxygen. He knows that to place the hand over the mouth during this process would hinder the flow, depriving the blood of essential oxygen.

24

He doesn't listen when she tells him where to find something, then hollers, "I can't find it. It's not here!"

Explanation:

This common curiosity occurs because of an inherent blindness possessed by the male.

This, if allowed to, can enhance a marriage by giving the female an extra sense of purpose, self-esteem, and an appreciation for the fact that she is so needed as his "helpmate." Remember, without Eve, Adam would never have found the forbidden fruit.

25

He chews with his mouth open.

Explanation:

Her good cooking shouldn't be hidden behind closed lips.

26

He rolls his socks together in a ball and puts them in the laundry basket.

Explanation:

Every man is aware that occasionally there may be a *very* slight hint of an odor in his socks. Rather than polluting other clothes in the hamper, he goes to the trouble of insulating them by rolling the socks into a tight ball.

Lloyd Maddoux was a pastor in hot and humid Kirbyville, Texas. He lived about 40 miles from his church, so he took two changes of clothing with him on Sundays, and during the day he would change clothes. As he spoke during one service, he reached into the top pocket of his jacket, grabbed what he thought was his handkerchief, and wiped his sweating brow. It was a sock that he had in his hand.

27

He puts half-eaten food back in the refrigerator.

Explanation:

Women don't understand such love. The male heart longs to share with others. It is for this reason that he doesn't consume *all* the food. This kindness isn't confined to refrigerated food. He may even go to the trouble of taking small bites out of chocolates in a box of candy. This is so that guests can see what flavor is inside.

> A woman in Norfolk, Virginia, should have put food in her refrigerator rather than in her pot-bellied pig. She faced up to $2,500 in fines and a year in jail for ignoring the veterinarian's warnings and overfeeding her porky pet. "Pinkie" should have weighed a maximum of 100 pounds, but this pot-belly's pot-belly scraped the ground at around 200 pounds. The pig was eventually captured by animal control officers, who laid a breadcrumb trail to their vehicle, and was put on a diet.

28

He doesn't discover a ketchup stain until he is due to go out.

Explanation:

Dried ketchup that has been spilled on clothing has a chameleon property—that is, until the moment before he is due to go out.

29

He takes "short cuts" that are longer.

Explanation:

Not only are these excursions memorable opportunities for his lovely wife to see different parts of the country, they are opportunities for different parts of the country to see his lovely wife.

30

He reads while she's speaking to him.

Explanation:

Men are normally able to absorb only one thing at a time. He understands that his wife is made differently. Her incredible brain is able to simultaneously process input from multiple sources. He wants to be like her. Therefore, he often attempts to do this while his wife is conversing with him.

31

He messes up the toothpaste.

Explanation:

The enlightened know that toothpaste has an inclination to mess itself up, even without his help. This is due to the law of entropy: "The irreversible tendency of a system, including the universe, toward increasing disorder."

32

He clicks ballpoint pens.

Explanation:

This may seem like an annoying, pointless actitivy. However, it is an important (and often neglected) form of digital exercise for the thumb.

33

He rattles keys or loose change in his pocket.

Explanation:

A shallow thinker may see this merely as a man rattling his keys. *However, there is something much more profound taking place.* Unless one is gifted with a musically sensitive ear, one will not appreciate the subtle hint of Beethoven or Mozart, in what the unlearned perceive as noise pollution. A woman who doesn't understand this may stop a man from rattling his keys, but his natural sense of rhythm will more than likely manifest itself in another manner. This may be in the form of rattling pocket change, drumming the fingers, or the ever-popular *rapid-heel movement*. This sometimes will cause "table tremors," if his leg is leaning against a table.

34
He taps his fingers.

Explanation:

Most of the great composers were men, who no doubt couldn't control the instinctive urge to let music manifest through their talented fingertips.

This is both "digital" music and an aerobic exercise for the fingers. It is important to keep a fivefold muscular balance, in light of explanation #32.

35

He sucks air through his teeth.

Explanation:

This also has wonderful symphonic potential, requiring constant practice because it is the most difficult of the body's natural instruments to finely tune. This rehearsal usually takes place at the conclusion of a meal, when he is feeling most relaxed and in the mood for music.

He *diligently* rehearses this skill, hoping that the day will come when he is able to rattle his keys, tap his fingers, and suck air through his teeth at the same time. This will bring together a symphony—a harmonizing, spine-tingling orchestral wonder that will make her proud to be the woman who patiently stood by her man during the many years of painful preparation.

This also results in less food flossed onto the mirror.

36

He will not turn the windshield wipers on until he can't see a thing in front of him.

Explanation:

The way to remove his wife's stress over his driving is to remove all sight of danger from her eyes.

Apparently a pastor in North Carolina couldn't see what was in front of him when he entered a restaurant restroom. He didn't notice the "Wo," which was on the door at a slight angle from the rest of the word. All he saw was the "...men." Inside, he found a small girl and, to his horror, saw a pair of lady's shoes under a stall door. He made a hasty exit, then waited in the men's restroom until he was sure the mother and child had left the scene. As he was sitting in the restaurant sometime later, he heard a child say, "That's the man, Mommy!"

37

He says, "Don't go on about it…"

Explanation:

This short phrase is sometimes misunderstood to be a reference to incessant nagging. It actually means, "Don't go on about it, sweetheart, until I am able to *fully* appreciate the incredible depth to which you are taking the subject."

In Phoenix, Arizona, a policeman pulled over a car for having tinted windows. He informed the driver that they were illegal, but said he would let her off with a warning. She insisted that she needed something in writing to convince her husband. He told her that she should tell him that they were against the law, and that he should replace them. But she wasn't happy with that. She continued to go on (and on) about the subject, saying that she needed something in writing. The officer then left for a moment and returned with "something in writing" for her—a traffic ticket.

38

He invites people to dinner without telling her.

Explanation:

He becomes so excited about her cooking that his mind enters a state of delirium, causing him to forget minor details about who's coming when.

39

He wakes her up to see if she's asleep.

Explanation:

Winston Churchill regularly used what is commonly called a "power nap." This is a sleep that may last for only a few minutes (or even seconds) but it results in the "napper" awakening refreshed.

Her husband simply wants her to rise to greatness, and he is therefore training her body to perfect the art of the "power nap."

40

He answers "Uh-huh" and "Hmmm" to everything.

Explanation:

A wise man speaks few words. Every statement he hears registers in his subconscious mind, and is being managed and then compartmentalized. His faculties are so deep that sometimes his conscious mind isn't even aware of this process. He is instinctively formulating wisdom that will one day manifest through his lips . . . and it may be only one wise word.

A woman in Norfolk, Virginia, heard more than a few words from her husband. Bruce Corson was on a flight to Chicago when there was a loud bang, and the co-pilot announced that he thought the nose wheel had blown off. Corson agonized over whether he should call his wife and upset her. If he did nothing, he may deny her the opportunity to hear his voice for the last time. When he finally made the call he didn't have the nerve to tell her about the plane's troubles. As he made small talk, she became upset with him for spending three dollars a minute just to say "Hello." Despite the loud bang, the plane landed safely.

41

He doesn't ask any details about the weight, sex, etc., when a friend has a baby.

Explanation:

The typically male "So your wife had a baby? Congratulations...Did you catch the game last night?" doesn't mean that the man isn't interested in the birth of a child. He is aware that sometimes men get things a little wrong. Rather than give his wife inaccurate details, he prefers that she get the particulars directly. This is because social information gathering is foreign to the male. Watch what happens when women encounter someone they haven't seen in quite some time. First, there is the high-pitched greeting: "Martha...*good to see you!*" Then comes the immediate information-gathering process: "How's Fred, the baby, the new house (etc.)?" The male language is different. Unlike women, men don't crave *depth* of social knowledge.

42

He leaves nail clippings on the bathroom sink and floor.

Explanation:

Nails have the ability to store an electrical charge, which nylon socks can produce. The synthetic nature of the material gives the nail a positive static charge, which is immediately drawn toward carpet (which has a negative charge) as soon as the nail is cut. Unfortunately, the nail's chameleon quality (the ability to change to the color of its surroundings) makes it impossible for the male eye to detect its location... *as much as he tries.*

43

He pokes his finger in her mouth when she yawns.

Explanation:

This is not (as some believe) motivated by an overwhelming urge to be annoying. The action is simply provoked by the same instinct that drives men to explore deep, dark caves.

44

He spills ketchup on his shirt or tie.

Explanation:

Women are often frustrated when time causes their favorite clothes to look worn and tatty. This dilemma is continually in the back of her husband's mind. He knows that when archaeologists have uncovered primeval clothing, it usually disintegrates when touched by human hands. However, it is well known that stained areas on the clothes remain intact.

What may look like a man who hasn't the brains to keep food off his clothing is actually a man who is working toward the good of all women. One happy day, when the right mixture of ketchup hits the right material and it is perfectly preserved, forever lifting his name high among the heroes of humanity, he will remember the many times he (in quiet humility) endured the scorn of unscientific minds.

45

He tells her he prefers the "old way" she cooks.

Explanation:

Maturity in marriage is often seen in the way a couple handles an argument. This growth can come only through experience. Even though his words *may* be interpreted as ingratitude, or as, "I *hate* this food," it is his way of gently "stirring" a discussion. This means that both the husband and the wife will gain valuable experience, causing positive growth in their relationship.

Dick Hayes, a pastor in San Antonio, Texas, decided to speak to the kids in his congregation about gratitude toward parents for the food they put in their mouths and the clothes they put on their backs. He directed his attention to the children and said, "You children should be grateful to your parents for the food they put on your backs..."

46

He reads billboard signs on the freeway out loud.

Explanation:

Too many drivers are involved in car wrecks because they don't concentrate on their driving. This is because their minds vegetate. They do nothing but stare at the road in front of them—which has a hypnotic effect. Wise men keep their minds active and alert by becoming involved in their surroundings.

In Wood Dale, Illinois, a man named Bob proposed to his girlfriend on a billboard with the words: "Teri, please marry me! Love, Bob." Over the following days, the billboard company received ten calls from women named Teri asking if it was their Bob.

47

He forgets their wedding anniversary.

Explanation:

When every day is better than the day before, the exhilaration and joy of daily marriage overloads the brain and makes history seem trivial compared to the present ecstasy.

48

He drives over bumps and potholes.

Explanation:

It may sound too good to be true, but this is a form of exercise that burns calories while the person remains seated. Not only do the actual bumps cause shaking of the body, thus dissolving unsightly excess, but also the facial heat that follows each bump dissipates throughout the body, burning additional fat.

The American Dietary Association has revealed that ten calories are ingested in the licking of a stamp, approximately the same amount as in a stick of celery. The U.S. Postal Service denies the claim. Some have suggested aggressive stamp licking burns off more calories than it puts on.

49

He leaves doors wide open on cold days.

Explanation:

Doors are deliberately left open so that the world can catch a glimpse of the most beautiful woman on earth.

50

He constantly "clicks" his fingernails.

Explanation:

This is his own personal "turn signal," an indication that he will soon be turning.

51

He gives her greetings from an old friend, whose name he forgot.

Explanation:

Men rarely forget anything. The problem is that the files in his mental database are so incredibly sophisticated and complex that they are very difficult to locate. This is why it's best to have a woman rather than a man witness a bank robbery. Most women can immediately recall a criminal down to the size and shape of his nose. Most men can hardly recollect if he even *had* a nose.

52

He buys flowers for his mother, when he hasn't bought his wife flowers for years.

Explanation:

In his pursuit of the adrenaline rush, this is another way he has of flirting with death (see explanation #9).

About 200 horrified people looked on as Kenny Cypress of Florida had his head trapped inside a 10-foot, 350-pound alligator for about two minutes. Friends wedged metal pipes in the alligator's mouth to free the man, who was taken to the hospital and released a few hours later with holes in his skull and face. Cypress, who had been putting his head inside the alligator for two weeks, said, "As long as you don't bump anything in there, you're okay. As soon as something touches the inside, you're in trouble. There's no way to keep the mouth from closing."

53

He gets food on his chin.

Explanation:

This doesn't mean that the man she married is an imbecile. Because men shave daily, the constant contact of the razor on the skin causes it to lose its sensitivity. Food particles—egg, cheese, butter, tomatoes, toast, meat, potatoes, hamburger, gravy, ketchup, etc.—stick to his chin (sometimes all at once), without him being at all aware of their presence.

54

He buys her gardening tools for Christmas.

Explanation:

He is secretly hoping that she buys him garden tools, so that they can share the mutual joy of working together in the garden.

55

He walks on the floor while she is cleaning it.

Explanation:

Even a dangerous wet floor can't keep him away from her.

A man who wanted to be close to his woman decided that he would be the first man to go over Niagara Falls in a barrel with his girlfriend. He spent $26,000 on a luxury barrel, complete with air tanks. He got his heart's desire after his brother kindly pushed the barrel over the falls. He then faced a fine of $26,000 for trespassing on private property.

56

He gets milk on his chin.

Explanation:

He has seen the popular celebrity milk campaign, and he is trying to impress his beloved.

57

He chews his food for two weeks before swallowing it.

Explanation:

Her cooking is too good to swallow. He wants to savor each delicious morsel as long as he can.

58

He puts the dog out when it's raining.

Explanation:

This is to clean the animal.

In Simi Valley, California, a man was charged with biting a police dog. When officers arrived at the man's home to arrest him for assaulting a 14-year-old boy, the animal was sent in to search for the man. The dog found him hiding in a closet, and was then bitten by the vicious beast.

59

He lets the dog in when it's raining.

Explanation:

Only when it's clean.

A man in Long Beach, California, found himself in court for throwing a dachshund off a bridge. After the lowly dog snapped at his child, the man snapped, and drove to a local bridge and tossed the doomed dog out of his car window. The dog swam to the shore and was no worse off for the ordeal. However, a passerby saw the incident and the dog-thrower found himself facing a charge of dog endangerment.

60

He writes down important phone messages or numbers that are unreadable.

Explanation:

This is his answer to the expensive and cumbersome paper shredder. He knows the damage that has been done when legible information has gotten into the wrong hands.

He also wants her to realize that being married to a doctor wouldn't be as wonderful as she may imagine.

61

He enters a room, turns the TV on, and then leaves the room.

Explanation:

This is to create a warm, inviting atmosphere for those who may enter the room.

62

He salts the table as well as his food.

Explanation:

The spreading of salt around a table is more than masculine ineptness. Salt is often used symbolically. It is "thrown over the shoulder," and people are often encouraged to take something "with a grain of salt" (this book, for example). Salt, spread about a table (or wherever) in a generous manner, is symbolic of a kind and generous soul.

63

He asks where something is in the cupboard, when it's close enough to bite him.

Explanation:

This is one of life's great mysteries that will hopefully one day be solved. It is an enigma in the category of UFOs and Elvis sightings. The object in question *wasn't there*... until the female pointed it out to him.

64

He greets the dog with more enthusiasm than he does his wife.

Explanation:

This happens simply because deep within the male subconscious there is a desire for his wife to greet him the way the dog does. He longs for his mate to run to meet him every time he comes home. He wants her to jump on him and kiss his face, with her eyes sparkling with unspeakable joy.

65

He kicks off his shoes in front of the TV, and leaves them where she will trip over them.

Explanation:

These are deliberately left close at hand in case of sudden fire or earthquake. Unsightly though they may be to his tidy mind, they are there so that he can speedily run through burning embers, or broken glass, to rescue her.

He wears his socks inside out.

Explanation:

Sometimes a man will even deliberately act like an idiot, just to make his wife feel assured that he needs her.

A pastor could have used a little help from his wife when they were driving from Nebraska to Stirling, Colorado. He was due to speak in a local church, so he quickly grabbed a shirt from a suitcase on the back seat, and his wife dropped him off at their hotel. Meanwhile, she had to go elsewhere. When he was changing into his good clothes, he found that he had grabbed his wife's blouse and not his shirt. He wore it to the meeting and nobody noticed. It must have been a men's *meeting.*

67

He doesn't notice her new hairstyle.

Explanation:

The natural beauty of her face captivates his entire attention.

68

He puts food in the microwave for three hours, and burns his mouth when he tries to eat it.

Explanation:

This is simply a method of controlling his calorie intake. A man who employs this technique is able (because of swollen lips and a burned tongue) to slow down the entire process of food consumption. This means he eats less.

69

He offers quick solutions to her complex problems.

Explanation:

This may be because the male brain is a sophisticated data processor, which has the uncanny ability to process information and then quickly spit out a solution. This is to be admired.

A pastor in Bakersfield, California, may have believed he found a quick solution for growing his congregation. He promised his church that if 300 people attended the services, he would kiss a pig during Sunday school. Unfortunately, this upset a number of his congregation and they left the church.

70

He falls asleep while she's talking.

Explanation:

Science has often flirted with the concept that the body may take in information while in the sleeping mode. Here is an example of a pioneer, a trailblazer—a man who may be misunderstood, even by his wife, as he experiments with this incredible mode of learning.

71

He never cleans the garage.

Explanation:

This is to give her extensive inventory for future yard sales. Also, time in the garage means time away from her…a horrifying thought.

In Connecticut, police arrested a man who was a traveling yard sale. They initially stopped his truck because of a noisy muffler, but inside they found a load of grenades, a rocket, bullets, bayonets, and daggers. After 15 homes were evacuated in the surrounding area, the arsenal of weapons was inspected and found to be "duds." The man ran a business where he purchased goods from self-storage renters who stopped making payments. Often he wasn't even aware of what he was buying. His loving sister said, "He's just a poor hardworking slob who has the worst luck."

He mentions an old girlfriend.

Explanation:

This is often mistaken for a common condition known as *ego-stupiditus.* However, with a little digging it will be discovered that he is trying to compare what "might have been" with the excellence he now has. He shudders at the thought of a near miss that would have trapped him into a dreadful life. It is similar to a happy rich man thinking back to the times in which he struggled as a poor, destitute youth.

73

He dominates the remote control.

Explanation:

Men like anything with buttons, knobs, and switches. Car manufacturers know this. The remote control has buttons that make things happen. This gives him a sense of power. For anyone else to have possession of the remote control (especially his wife) means that he is *not* in control. *This is a frightening thought for any man.*

74

He has the television too loud.

Explanation:

The slightly higher volume of the TV is so that people in another room, house, or in another neighborhood may appreciate the excitement of the program.

> *In Minnesota, a pastor was jailed for failing to show up for a court hearing after a neighbor complained that his praise and worship services were too loud. Noise pollution instruments measured the service noise level and found that it was equivalent to a low-flying jet plane.*

75

He channel surfs.

Explanation:

Think of the shape and appearance of the brain. It *looks* like a sponge. This is because it *is* a sponge. Like a parched sponge, the masculine mind craves liquid knowledge. It cannot remain dry; it must seek and absorb. Man is able to do this by merely looking at a channel for an instant, then moving on. This is what separates man from the beasts.

There is another explanation for why a man channel surfs. It has been said that this has to do with his *hunting instincts*. He hunts through the channels, his "gun" in hand, like a man after fleeing prey. When he sees something he doesn't like, he simply "shoots" it and moves on.

76

He tells people stories that he has already told them.

Explanation:

Notice that he usually does this with men (see explanation #2).

77

He doesn't shave when he goes out.

Explanation:

This is another example of selflessness. He does this purely for contrast with his wife. His thorny face will make hers look like a beautiful rose.

One man who cared about how he looked in public was a criminal well-known for continually shining his shoes. While breaking into a house, he scraped a shoe as he crawled through the window. After stealing the goods, he stopped to shine his shoes, but accidentally dropped his shining rag—which had his name on it. He was promptly arrested.

78

He flosses food particles onto the bathroom mirror.

Explanation:

He knows that his loving wife wants him to take care of his dental hygiene. With a quick glance at the mirror each morning, she can easily see that he is dutifully flossing.

79

He doesn't notice her new dress.

Explanation:

A man's powers of observation go beyond the mere external. Therefore, his admiration for the inner gifts of her character blinds him to the outer wrapping.

In Bellflower, California, a youth leader sat in the front pew of a church dressed in a bright blue suit as "Bible Bird." He was eagerly waiting to promote Vacation Bible School. Unfortunately, the pastor's powers of observation weren't working that day. He forgot all about the promotion. The young man sat through the whole service as "Bible Bird" and left at the end without having made the announcement.

80

He wears light socks with a dark suit.

Explanation:

It is common knowledge that trendsetters are never admired until after the fact. In the meantime, they must endure ridicule.

A man who was a trendsetter in Fort Myers, Florida, robbed a bank while wearing a deflated beach ball over his head. He had made holes for his eyes, and was cleverly wearing plastic bags over his hands. Apparently, this was the first case of its kind.

81

He doesn't read instructions when assembling things.

Explanation:

M en know that the instructions are to be referred to only when something goes wrong. They are the *final* alternative. This is because they are aware that people who don't speak English have written them, and the instructions need their own instruction book to make them understandable.

In 1991, a pastor should have read his linguistic instruction book a little more closely. He was visiting a town near Mexico City. It was very crowded, so he found himself saying, "Excuse me" in Spanish to those he bumped into. He was, however, getting strange looks from each person to whom he said the phrase. He found out later that he was actually saying, "Please spit on me." Both phrases sound similar in Spanish.

82

He leaves used dental floss lying around the house.

Explanation:

This is another amazing display of his thoughtfulness. The floss is for others to use.

83

He flushes the toilet while she's showering.

Explanation:

This is a very common "hot flash" experienced by many women. He does this for his wife's health because he knows that mildly scalding water can kill bacteria on the skin. Also, the sound of her high-pitched voice lets him know that his beloved is still in the land of the living. *This warms his ever-loving heart.*

84

He leaves things unwrapped in the refrigerator.

Explanation:

Many times a lid has been removed or food unwrapped revealing a disgusting mold growing on its surface. This happens only because the provisions have not been left in view. *It is for the well-being of his family* that he purposely leaves food visible. This is so a fungus may be detected immediately and be promptly removed from the refrigerator.

A man in Concord, California, took something unwrapped from his refrigerator. He showed up at the local police station with a frozen pigeon in his lunch box. When the low-flying racing pigeon smashed into the man's windshield on the freeway, he retrieved the bird, froze it as evidence, and presented it to the local police, with the view of seeking reparations from its owner. The officer who took the report said he tried to keep a straight face, but kept looking around for "Candid Camera."

85

He completely changes the subject of conversation to something he wants to talk about.

Explanation:

This is his attempt to build strength of character into his wife. He knows how hard the world can be. He is teaching her to remain strong, to keep her course in the stormy art of conversation. Powerful winds making a tree send its roots deep into the soil. *He is being her powerful wind.*

86

He says, "What have you been doing all day while I've been working?"

Explanation:

Interpretation: "My workload is nothing compared to what you have to do each day. Did you find a moment to relax, sweetheart?"

87

He doesn't put things back where he found them.

Explanation:

Women often have urges to completely rearrange a room. Men have not yet developed that gift to the extent of relocating an entire room. They begin with single objects.

On June 9, 1978, a cameraman couldn't put things back where he found them. Mr. Bob Specas was attempting to topple 100,000 dominoes in one go at the famed Manhattan Center in New York. Tension was high as he laid down more than 97,500 dominoes. All that remained was for Bob to lay down a mere 2,300 more and he would break the record. It was just then that the TV cameraman dropped his press badge and set them off.

88

He's lived there for years, yet still opens the wrong cupboards.

Explanation:

To the untrained eye, this may look as though he is an idiot, mistakenly opening the wrong cupboard every day. *But this action is deliberate.* He is gaining profound joy by seeing what lies inside the cupboard on his way to find the right item. A woman may find the same joy by gazing at her flower garden every day. He daily opens the dish cupboard en route to the glasses, simply to gaze at the plates.

He makes a joke when she is saying something serious.

Explanation:

Selfless husband that he is, he is willing to risk the loss of his teeth, just to see hers in a smile.

Two men found little to joke about in the following hunting incident, reported by a Michigan radio station. The two men decided to go duck hunting on a frozen lake, and loaded their new $30,000 van with their dog, guns, and beer. They drove onto the ice and decided to blast a hole in it to place their decoys to attract ducks. Of course, they moved far from their expensive new van, lit the fuse on a stick of dynamite, and threw it onto the ice. Their highly trained dog promptly ran after the dynamite. The men panicked, waving their arms and yelling at the dog. The animal, cheered on by their cries, picked up the dynamite and ran toward them. One of the men grabbed his gun and shot at the dog. The animal became confused and ran under the $30,000 vehicle with the dynamite still in its mouth. Both the van and the dog were blown to pieces.

90

He buys her useless gadgets for the kitchen.

Explanation:

These are more items for her future yard sales as well as interesting "conversation pieces."

91

He slurps milk straight from the cereal bowl.

Explanation:

This is the tendency of kings.

92

He gets shavings all over the bathroom counter when cleaning his razor.

Explanation:

H e likes to leave little romantic "reminders" of himself in the house for his beloved to find during the day.

93

He picks his teeth with his finger, in front of company.

Explanation:

He is searching for any leftover morsels of her succulent cooking.

94

He subscribes to a well-known geographic magazine and never looks at it.

Explanation:

The *piles* of magazines block out the unsightliness of his shoes that have been left lying around on the living room floor (see explanation #65).

95

He drives too fast.

Explanation:

Awoman has a right to feel a certain amount of apprehension when her husband drives their car. Her thought is, "This is the man who forgets names, doesn't listen when he's talked to, is blind when it comes to finding things in the cupboard. This is the one who reads billboards when he should be watching the road, spends most of his time dreaming about other things when driving, . . . *and he's in control of the vehicle!*"

While she may think he isn't in control, he has one eye on her ever-moving right foot. This foot (which shifts back and forth over an invisible brake pedal with every potential accident) is his clear indication of any impending danger. He also has an ear open to her frequent warnings about the many dangers she sees on the road, sidewalk, or driveways—as well as fields, parks, etc.—that apparently he doesn't see.

A man in California tried to convince a judge that he was driving 87 mph because that was the exact speed needed to aerate his aquarium. He maintained that that speed kept the fish alive as he moved the aquarium and his belongings from his former residence. The judge wasn't impressed.

96

He drives too slowly.

Explanation:

This often happens when he *appears* to be dreaming (see explanation #5).

In Houston, Texas, when a car thief passed a patrol car, the police gave chase. The panicking man realized that his car was too slow compared to the police vehicle, so he pulled over and tried to outrun the officers on foot. Unfortunately for him, he was wearing a seat belt, and as he sprang from the car his leg became entangled in the belt, and there he remained until he was arrested.

He tailgates.

Explanation:

A man is acutely aware of a woman's need for details. He realizes that there are few things in life more frustrating than not being able to clearly read the fine wording on bumper stickers on the vehicle in front.

98

He spends an hour in the shower.

Explanation:

This is another example of self-sacrifice. Incredibly, the shower has the ability to take him into his creative mode (see explanation #8). Who knows what great benefits have been given to women (the microwave, the hair dryer, etc.) because a man has denied himself and deliberately stayed in his creative mode? This precious time he devotes to the good of humanity can often be recognized by the sound of singing. It is a great mistake to holler, *"How long are you going to stay in there?"* or to threaten to run the cold water.

99

He stuffs towels on the towel rack, rather than hanging them.

Explanation:

O nly in recent years has the human race begun to understand the importance of conservation. One aspect of this is *space* conservation. As much as he realizes that it does look better to have one towel neatly spread on a rack, wisdom tells him that the "stuff method" can fit three or four towels in the equivalent space.

100

After a 30-minute phone conversation, when asked what his friend talked about he says, "Nothin' much."

Explanation:

Nothin' much" made it into the inner ear (see explanation #2).

101

He suggests writing a book called "101 Things Wives Do to Annoy Their Husbands."

Explanation:

He's just kidding. He knows in his heart that there wouldn't be enough material for such a publication. Besides, he wouldn't live long enough to finish the book.

How to Make Your Marriage Blossom

Thereis an interesting T-shirt for men that reads "Real men don't need instructions." That helps explain why I feel physically sick whenever I hold an instruction book in my hands. This is because they are usually published by the Department of Confusion.

I remember once buying a gadget from a magic shop. It looked like a cake of soap, but underneath it was a spring-loaded surprise. When it was picked up by some unsuspecting soul, it exploded... *really* loud. I purchased it for my teenaged nephew who was coming to stay at our house.

I decided to try it on my 18-year-old son *before* I sprung it on my nephew. I carefully pulled the spring back, slipped in the tiny gunpowder cap, and put it in his bathroom.

I then casually said, "Daniel, go into the bathroom and wash your hands." He stopped what he was doing and walked into the bathroom without a question. I waited with baited breath. Any second there was going to be a loud bang...*and a scream*. I waited for about 30 seconds. No bang and no scream. Something was wrong, so I walked into the bathroom and picked up the "soap." It had failed to explode. *I should have read the stupid instructions.*

I carefully turned it over and touched the spring. Suddenly there was a massive bang right in my face. It echoed around the bathroom walls, so loud that my ears rang. My son looked at me for a moment with a blank expression. Then he mumbled, "Roadrunner..." and stepped out of the bathroom.

Millions must feel a little like the coyote in the "Roadrunner." They think they are doing everything right in their marriage, but it explodes in their face. What a tragedy this is, with broken homes, ruined lives, and scarred children. All this happens simply because the "Instruction Book" is not being read.

What nation comes to mind when we hear the words "God and country"? Most of us think of the United States. We should. No other nation has the phrase "In God we trust" on its currency. The Ten Commandments adorn the walls of the Supreme Court. Our politicians open Congress in prayer.

When there was a call to remove "under God" from the Pledge of Allegiance, an ABC/Washington Post poll reported that an incredible 84% wanted "under God" to remain in the pledge. Most towns have churches on almost every corner.

Marriage vows were originally directed toward God. This is why I trust you won't be offended if I share with you principles from the Bible, the "Instruction Book," that have made our marriage work. At present, Sue and I have been married for more than 66 years (33 each) and we have found that the key to a good marriage is for husbands to love their wives "as Christ loved the church." You may not be familiar with this phrase, so I will try to explain its meaning. To do so, we're going to have to go all the way back to the Book of Exodus.

Our Dilemma

We are told in the Bible, "There is none good, no not one." Yet, from our point of view, there are *many* good people. The problem is that God sees humanity from another perspective. His definition of "good" is moral perfection—*in thought, word, and deed.*

God's standard of morality is revealed in the Ten Commandments. To see how much "Christ loved the church," we will briefly go through the Commandments and compare them to our standards:

The First Commandment is, "You shall have no other gods before Me." That means we should put God first in our affections.

The Second Commandment is, "You shall not make for yourself a graven image." This command means that we shouldn't make a god in our own image, either with our hands or with our minds. I was guilty of this. I had made a god to suit myself. My god didn't have any moral dictates. In truth, my god didn't exist. He was a figment of my imagination, shaped to conform to my sins.

The Third Commandment is, "You shall not take the name of the Lord your God in vain, for the Lord will not hold him guiltless who takes His name in vain." Have we ever used God's name as a cuss word?

The Fourth Commandment is, "Remember the Sabbath day, to keep it holy." I ignored this command for 22 years of my non-Christian life. Not for a second did I say, "God gave me life; what does He therefore require of me?"

The Fifth is, "Honor your father and mother." We are commanded to value our parents implicitly, in a way that is pleasing in the sight of God.

The Sixth Commandment is, "You shall not murder." Jesus warned that if we get angry without cause, we are in danger of judgment. If we hate our brother, God calls us a murderer.

The Seventh is, "You shall not commit adultery." However, Jesus warned, "Whoever looks upon a woman to lust after her, has committed adultery already with her in his heart."

The Eighth Commandment says, "You shall not steal." Have we ever taken something that belonged to someone else (regardless of its value)?

The Ninth Commandment is, "You shall not bear false witness." Have we ever told a fib, a "white" lie, a half-truth, or an exaggeration? Then we have borne false witness. How many lies do you have to tell to be a liar? Just one.

The final nail in our coffin is, "You shall not covet." That means we should not desire things that belong to others. Who hasn't done that?

Way back in 1972, when I was confronted with these Commandments, I suddenly understood that if God judged me by them on Judgment Day, I would be guilty and would end up in hell. How did you do? Are you innocent or guilty? The Bible tells us, "There is none righteous, no not one; there is none that understands, there is none that seeks after God."

Herein is Love

Here now is *how much* "Christ loved the church." Each of us is guilty before God. The Bible makes it clear that on the Day of Judgment, if God were to give us justice, we would all end up in hell. That's what we deserve from His perspective. But God is rich in mercy. He sent His Son to suffer and die for our sins. When Jesus was on the cross, He took the punishment for the sin of the world—"He was bruised for our iniquities." The Bible says, "Herein is love, not that we loved God, but that he loved us, and sent his Son to be the propitiation [a substitute] for our sins." Then Jesus rose from the dead, defeating death. He purchased everlasting life for all those who repent and trust in Him. That's *how much* Christ loved the church. He gave His life for it . . . and that's how much a man should strive to love his wife. If a man is able to do that, she will almost certainly respond to him in a positive, loving way. Personally, I didn't possess such a selfless love until I became a Christian. If you are interested in everlasting life, and access to a selfless love, here's a model prayer of salvation for you to pray:

"Dear God, I have broken your Commandments. I have sinned against You. You have seen my every thought and deed. You saw the sins of my youth and unclean desires of my heart. I am truly sorry. I now understand how serious my transgressions have been. If justice was to be done and all of my sins uncovered on the

Day of Judgment, I know I would be guilty and justly end up in hell. Words cannot express my gratitude for the substitutionary death and resurrection of the Lord Jesus Christ. Please give me a selfless love. I will read the Bible daily, and obey what I read. In Jesus' name I pray, amen."

I trust that you now have more of an understanding of *how much* Christ loved the church. Our striving to love each other will be in direct proportion to our understanding of how much He loved the church. The more clearly we see our sinfulness, the more clearly we will see the depth of His great love —and the more willing we will be to extend that same love to others.

Five Principles for a Stronger Marriage

As I previously mentioned, Sue and I have a wonderful marriage. This is because we have put into practice certain biblical principles that I'd like to share with you. I will leave out Bible references so you won't feel as though you are being sermonized (these have been adapted from my book *God Doesn't Believe in Atheists*).

First (this one is for Christians), establish a regular prayer life *together*. If you are in a high-rise building and there's a fire, the correct response is to drop to your knees. Because smoke rises, you will see more clearly from that position and will avoid the poisonous fumes. Make your prayer-life so second nature to you both that the moment you find yourself in the fires of tribulation, you will drop to your knees. You will see more on the knees of prayer than through the thick and confusing smoke of misfortune.

Second, aim to rid yourself of a selfish human nature. A humble, "broken" spirit is found in one who is no longer living for himself. I've counseled enough marriages to know what causes all breakups: it is simply a philosophy of "Not your will, but mine be done." Having a broken spirit means giving up your rights for the rights of your spouse. Don't be like the wife who told her marriage counselor, "It all started on our wedding day—when he wanted to be in the wedding photos!" Don't do anything "through selfish ambition or conceit, but in lowliness of mind let each esteem others better than himself."

Third, make certain resolutions:

- Never mention the word "divorce" during an argument. The word should shock us. The more it is used as an argumentative weapon, the less distasteful it will seem. Avoid statements such as, "Sometimes I can really understand why some marriages end in divorce." If you both resolve that divorce is never an option, you will be motivated to work harder at having a good marriage.

- Vow not to let your emotions lead you to say things you will regret. You are most vulnerable to the one you confide in most—spouses know how to hurt each other. If you feel unable to restrain your sharp tongue in an argument, wait until you have cooled off and can talk reasonably.

- Learn how to say, "I'm sorry." Often I say I'm sorry not because I think I was in the wrong, but because the argument started in the first place. A wife testified at the closing of divorce proceedings, "It all started when he walked out and slammed the door." The husband butted in, "I didn't slam the door!" It was discovered that the wind had caught it. If only forgiveness and humility had been there the day that happened, rather than presumption and pride.

- Be aware of your own faults. Remember the proverb, "All the ways of a man are pure in his own eyes." The husband who says, "I have never made a mistake" has a wife who made a big one.

- Agree never to argue in front of your children. You will lose their respect, cause them to question the security of their home, and ruin your reputation in front of those most important to you.

- Don't let the sun go down on your anger. Don't "sleep on it," because it will fester and eventually poison you.

Fourth, show love and respect toward each other. Although some with the "Women's Liberation" mentality believe that the biblical husband/wife relationship is one of a master and a well-trained dog, they couldn't be further from the truth. The Bible does speak of women as the "weaker vessel," which is true physically. However, the biblical order is: as a strong, thorny stem upholds the tender, easily bruised, sweet-smelling rose, so should the husband uphold, love, and respect his wife. When you study a rose, notice how the leaves reach from the stem and embrace the delicate flower. So the arms of the husband should embrace his wife. That is God's order.

Again, the Bible commands husbands, "Love your wives, just as Christ also loved the church and gave Himself for her." Men will obey this only to the extent that they understand how much Christ loved the church. I once spoke at a men's camp to about eighty men, and told them that if they treated their wives sacrificially like this, they would no doubt be rewarded by their wives in a way that all men enjoy. For the next several seconds, you could have heard a pin drop. Suddenly one man, voicing the thought of the entire group, hollered, "Alright!" The room erupted with spontaneous joy, laughter, and loud amens. Ladies, if your husband doesn't open the car door for you when you get home at night, stay in the car until he does. If, however, you see the bedroom light switch off, give up and try again another time. Husbands, if you know what's good for you, show respect for your wife. It *will* become mutual, and you will be rewarded. You will reap what you sow, and thus enrich and lift your marriage.

Lastly, communicate. The Bible says that when a man and woman are joined in marriage, they "become one flesh." Sue and I met while we were working in a bank. At work we were called "the budgies" because we used to sit together each day and I would peck at her lunch. Nothing has changed. Not only is Sue my wife, but she's my best friend.

Think on this sobering thought, husbands. If the mute button worked on your wife as well as it does on the TV, and she was talking during the news, at which one would you aim the remote? You will always have news to listen to, so don't take for granted that you will always have your wife to keep you company. Communication is the glue that keeps the marriage bond strong.

I hope I have made you smile as I have tried to explain why men do the things they do to annoy women. Most of the things I have spoken of are born out of personal experience. I wrote a book called *101 of the Dumbest Things People Have Done*. One-third of the book is stupid things that *I* have done. One lady wrote to say that she laughed and laughed. She also enclosed a sympathy card for Sue.

A man once said to his wife, "I don't know how you can be so stupid and so beautiful at the same time." The wife responded, "Allow me to explain. God made me beautiful so you would be attracted to me; God made me stupid so I would be attracted to you."

If we men *really* want to improve our marriages, we should go through all 101 of the dumb things we do to annoy our wives, and begin to clean up our act. We should floss away from the mirror, and pick up nail clippings no matter what pain it causes the male mind. We should listen when she speaks, put down the newspaper for a moment, unroll the socks, drive a little slower (or faster), yield the remote contr... (perhaps that's going too far).

These things won't come naturally. There is, however, one powerful thought to help us remember why men should be the ones who change:

God made man from dirt.
For the woman He used prime rib.

Ten Final Tips on
How to Keep a Wife Happy

10. Don't eat mashed potatoes with your fingers.

9. Don't apologize too early after an argument, with, "Sorry, babe; I was wrong. So what's for dinner?"

8. Don't throw the baby in the air under a ceiling fan.

7. Don't fix dirty things in clean clothes.

6. Don't try to kiss her with a toothpick in your mouth.

5. Don't floss your teeth while driving.

4. Don't drive with your knees while putting your seat belt on.

3. Don't put your dirty clothes back in the closet.

2. Don't tell her that if you were Solomon, she would be in the top ten.

1. Don't try to start "the wave" at a funeral.

For a complete list of books, tapes, DVDs, videos, etc., by Ray Comfort, see www.livingwaters.com.